Introduction

Massimo Stanzione's painting of the beheading of John the Baptist

That Jesus of Nazareth (ca. 4 BC-30 CE) was crucified is the closest to a historical fact anyone can say about him. Biblical scholars have spent centuries debating the details of what Jesus did and said, but this crude fact - that Jesus suffered capital punishment at the hands of the Roman authority by crucifixion - is accepted by the overwhelming majority of scholars. That there once was a cross where Jesus suffered and died is, therefore, the sequential logical affirmation.

Jesus's destiny was not uncommon. Indeed, many other Jews perished were nailed to a wooden cross on the outskirts of Jerusalem (thousands, according to the historian Josephus, who was an eyewitness to the great Jewish revolt against Rome). The cross, a symbol of failure and shame for those who died on it and their families, was considered, from the dawn of Christianity, as the climactic moment in the career of its Messiah: His crucifixion and the ascension to His throne as the true king of the Jews. Hence, once the persecution against Christianity was over, and after enough time had passed, those who were interested began to search for the truth in the evidence.

In many respects, none of this should be surprising because holy relics can be found in many different religions, whether Christian, pagan, Hindu, or Buddhist. A relic is defined as something directly associated with a revered saint, teacher, ancestor, or some miraculous manifestation of deity in the material world. A relic and a reliquary are two types of sacramental tools. A reliquary is a container or

About Charles River Editors

Charles River Editors is a boutique digital publishing company, specializing in bringing history back to life with educational and engaging books on a wide range of topics. Keep up to date with our new and free offerings with this 5 second sign up on our weekly mailing list, and visit Our Kindle Author Page to see other recently published Kindle titles.

We make these books for you and always want to know our readers' opinions, so we encourage you to leave reviews and look forward to publishing new and exciting titles each week.

Christian Relics and the Arma Christi: The History of the Medieval Search for Relics Related to the Passion of Christ

By Charles River Editors

Giotto's painting of the crucifixion

Introduction

Massimo Stanzione's painting of the beheading of John the Baptist

That Jesus of Nazareth (ca. 4 BC-30 CE) was crucified is the closest to a historical fact anyone can say about him. Biblical scholars have spent centuries debating the details of what Jesus did and said, but this crude fact - that Jesus suffered capital punishment at the hands of the Roman authority by crucifixion - is accepted by the overwhelming majority of scholars. That there once was a cross where Jesus suffered and died is, therefore, the sequential logical affirmation.

Jesus's destiny was not uncommon. Indeed, many other Jews perished were nailed to a wooden cross on the outskirts of Jerusalem (thousands, according to the historian Josephus, who was an eyewitness to the great Jewish revolt against Rome). The cross, a symbol of failure and shame for those who died on it and their families, was considered, from the dawn of Christianity, as the climactic moment in the career of its Messiah: His crucifixion and the ascension to His throne as the true king of the Jews. Hence, once the persecution against Christianity was over, and after enough time had passed, those who were interested began to search for the truth in the evidence.

In many respects, none of this should be surprising because holy relics can be found in many different religions, whether Christian, pagan, Hindu, or Buddhist. A relic is defined as something directly associated with a revered saint, teacher, ancestor, or some miraculous manifestation of deity in the material world. A relic and a reliquary are two types of sacramental tools. A reliquary is a container or box for a relic, allowing it to be displayed to the public and thus transfer its powers to magical and liturgical works. There is another definition of a relic: anything that would be a miraculous manifestation of a deity in the material world. In Christianity, there are countless numbers of relics, most of them being associated with Jesus Christ.

In the early years of Christianity, it was forbidden to move and share the remains of saints and martyrs, and they were protected so that their final resting places, such as catacombs and cemeteries, remained intact. The earliest recorded Christian relics, specifically the bones and ashes of martyrs, date from the 2nd century. 200 years later, St. Ambrose and others set out to dig up the corpses and honor them. At that time, it was considered that every holy body could be dismembered and divided among the faithful to worship it. The remains of corpses sometimes came into someone else's hands as a gift, and sometimes they were stolen. At one point, the demand for holy bodies was such that bodyguards were assigned to dying saints to prevent their bodies from being dismembered after death.[1]

---

[1] Andrew Butterfield, "What Remains," The New Republic, June 28, 2023,

The veneration of the relics of saints was so common among the faithful because they believed saints in Heaven interceded for believers on Earth. As a result, numerous healings and miracles were attributed to the relics, and many stories and myths about miracles arose from these beliefs. By word of mouth, the stories spread among the faithful, and finally, they were recorded in books of hagiographies such as *The Golden Legend* by Jacobus de Voragine. Inevitably, the demand for relics grew with the popularization of stories about their miracles, so a rich trade in relics developed indirectly.

The use of relics, perhaps the greatest superstition, reveals the deception and inconsistency that Christians have been subjected to for centuries. Parts of the True Cross were among the most worshipped relics, but there were so many of them scattered across Europe and other parts of the world that Calvin once joked that if all the pieces were collected, they would form a shipload, despite the fact the cross was only large enough that one person could carry it. To get around this conundrum,

https://newrepublic.com/article/92804/medieval-christian-art-relics.

figures like St. Paulinus spoke of the reintegration of the cross, in other words claiming that the cross never diminished, no matter how many pieces were broken off from it.[2]

Arma Christi is a collective name for objects, devices, and symbols related to the Passion of Christ. They are also called tools of Christ or instruments of suffering. They have often been depicted in art, iconography, Christian symbolism, and piety, and they had a particularly high value in the Middle Ages. Their purpose was to arouse a feeling of gratitude to Christ for the gift of redemption.

In the narrow sense of the word, *arma Christi* referred to 10 such objects, but with the spread of devotion to the Way of the Cross and the veneration of Christ's Passion, the number of such objects multiplied, and in time people began applying the term to scenes and even people. Aside from the True Cross, one of the most poignant visuals in the Passion is the Crown of Thorns, and another relic

[2] Holy scripture and traditions of the Eastern Orthodox Church, accessed June 26, 2023, https://gospelfororthodox.files.wordpress.com/2013/03/holy-scripture-and-traditions-of-the-eastern-orthodox-church.pdf.

considered priceless was the Virgin Mary's Girdle.

Legends aside, the real problem arises when historians eliminate the mythical elements and try to identify how and when these relics appeared for the first time in history, and from there, follow them from generation to generation and from church to church, through the hands of kings and popes. It is a long and complicated history, from believers of Christianity to its enemies, and historians have to try to determine how the relics were lost and recovered, how they were scattered all over the world (and only sometimes reunited again), how they were stolen by invading armies and used as impressive forms of propaganda; and even how they were lost, recovered, and deposited in the places where they are venerated today. Some would even argue that the history of some of these relics, and the tumult they gave rise to, are more exciting than the question of their authenticity.

Christian Relics and the Arma Christi: The History of the Medieval Search for Relics Related to the Passion of Christ

About Charles River Editors

Introduction

Accounts of Jesus and the Crucifixion

"Now it was the third hour, and they crucified him. And the inscription of his accusation was written above: *The King of the Jews*. With him they also crucified two robbers, one on his right and the other on his left." - Mark 15: 25-27

On Nisan 14 in the year 30 CE, according to the best estimates, a rural man from Galilee was executed outside the walls of Jerusalem in a place called Golgotha, along with two other rebels under the specific charge of sedition. He was executed for proclaiming himself the King of the Jews, clearly a high treason under Roman rule. The name of the convicted was Jesus of Nazareth, and around him, a movement that would soon become Christianity had begun to take form.

The life of Jesus was documented in meticulous detail in the New Testament, primarily the four biographies written by early Christians: the evangelists Matthew, Mark, Luke and John, and one obstacle is that it's unclear whether historians and scholars can truly learn more about Jesus than contemporaries who were there to hear the preaching, see the crucifixion, and then write their teacher's biography.

The problem is precisely that the Gospels are not biographies, were not written by eyewitnesses, and were not four separate reports; instead, they comprise a tradition in evolution. The Gospel of Mark, which was composed using scattered writings around the year 68, was used by Matthew and Luke decades later, who also inserted in their own Gospels now lost documents and other stories about Jesus that circulated orally, to which the author of Mark had no access. Skeptics will wonder whether it's possible to know with absolute certainty anything about Jesus if the information that has come down to the modern day was manipulated both by individuals and the early Church.

As a result, any biography of Jesus must start with the most basic question: that of his actual historical existence. There is no indisputable, archaeological evidence that proves the existence of Jesus of Nazareth.[i] Not a single monument inscription or picture of his time (first century CE) refers to him. The earliest fragments of codex or papyrus that mention Jesus date from the early second century, a hundred years after his ministry took place. The oldest complete copies of the New Testament date from the fourth century. That has nothing to do, of course, with their date of composition, which is earlier. Much earlier. One might wonder how it's possible that, besides the Gospels and the Epistles, no other author of the first century mentions a man who, according to tradition, raised the dead, turned water into wine, walked on water and multiplied bread and fish. Wouldn't men like Seneca, or Philo of Alexandria or Tiberius, the emperor himself, have marveled if they had heard about him? Probably yes, but then we aren't considering that, in his time and place, Jesus was a nobody; he was, in fact, a marginal Jew, as Biblical scholar John P. Meier calls him, living in a marginal province, teaching in illiterate and secondary towns like Capernaum, Nazareth and Chorazin.

Either way, the assertion that there's no independent evidence of this time isn't entirely true, although some of it might be based on his followers' reports. There is almost unanimous agreement among Biblical scholars that two of them are indeed reports of the 1st century, written not by Christians but by independent observers, who confirm the existence of Jesus as a historical figure.

The first and most important textual evidence is in *Antiquities of the Jews*, a book by historian Flavius Josephus, who was not a Christian. Josephus was born around the year 35 and was a military leader in Galilee during the first major Jewish revolt against Rome in the year 66 CE. He witnessed the destruction of Jerusalem in 70 CE and composed his various volumes in the last quarter of the first century. He lived and wrote at the same time as the authors of the Gospels. Josephus is essential for those who want to know the history of Israel during the 1st century, and he is one of the few non-Christian sources where we can find authentic reports about well-known figures like Herod, John the Baptist, Pilate, the high priest Caiaphas and Jesus of Nazareth, who is mentioned twice in *Antiquities of the Jews*.

A bust of Josephus

The best-known mention is the one known as *Testimonium Flavianum*. Found in Book 18, Chapter 3 of Josephus's work, it says, "About this time there lived Jesus, a wise man, *if indeed one ought to call him a man*. For he was one who performed surprising deeds and was a teacher of such people as accept the truth gladly. He won over many Jews and many of the Greeks. *He was the*

Messiah. And when, upon the accusation of the principal men among us, Pilate had condemned him to a cross, those who had first come to love him did not cease. He appeared to them spending a third day restored to life, for the prophets of God had foretold these things and a thousand other marvels about him. And the tribe of the Christians, so called after him, has still to this day not disappeared."

Despite what the passage says, in the form it has come down over the centuries, it presents critical problems. First, Josephus was not a follower of Jesus and couldn't have possibly written that "he was the Messiah," so it's very likely that the paragraph is authentic but suffered several interpolations at the hands of Christian copyists. Although there's no absolute agreement, the majority of scholars concedes that the testimony contains interpolations (*in italics above*) and that by removing them, they can recover the original testimony, which would look like this: "About this time there lived Jesus, a wise man, for he was one who performed surprising deeds and was a teacher of such people as accept the truth gladly. He won over many Jews and many of the Greeks. And when, upon the accusation of the principal men among us, Pilate had condemned him to a cross, those who had first come to love him did not cease. And the tribe of the Christians, so called after him, has still to this day not disappeared."

The paragraph in this form is neutral and flows more naturally without the suspected interpolations, and it also corresponds to the style of Josephus. The testimony appears in one part of the book where he describes various calamities that happened in the country during the reign of Emperor Tiberius. Among other reasons that support its authenticity, Josephus calls the Christians a "tribe," a term that never appears in the New Testament or the patristic writings; he mentions that Jesus attracted many Gentiles, something the evangelists don't mention either. Most importantly, he's pointing to Rome and not to the Jews as the ones responsible for the death of this man, which constitutes a very different point of view from those of the Gospels, and is perhaps closer to the historical truth.

A bust of Tiberius

The second testimony that appears in *Antiquities of the Jews* is less spectacular, but unlike the previous one, this one is decisively and unanimously accepted as authentic. It comes later in the book, when Josephus describes certain atrocities committed by the high priest Ananias during a power vacuum. "Festus was now dead, and Albinus was but upon the road; so he (the High Priest) assembled the Sanhedrin of judges, and brought before them the brother of Jesus, who was called Christ, whose name was James, and some others; and when he had formed an accusation against them as breakers of the law, he delivered them to be stoned." St. James's execution is not reported in the New Testament, but it's important to note that Josephus mentions Jesus in passing, only to identify St. James with language that a Christian copyist would never have used ("Jesus, who was called Christ," or "Jesus the so-called Christ"). That speaks strongly in favor of the paragraph's authenticity. Even those who doubt the accuracy of Josephus's first mention of Jesus accept the second. Therefore, this is the best independent testimony about his existence as an historical figure.

Another report that most historians (although fewer than in the previous case) take as genuine and independent, is the one from Tacitus (approx. 56-117), an historian of the Roman Empire whose *Annals* go from the death of emperor Augustus in 15 CE to the death of Domitian in 76 CE, thus covering the years of Jesus's ministry and the early Christian movement. Tacitus was a rigorous historian who put great care in his sources. As a senator, he had access to Roman official records (the proceedings of the Senate and the acts of the government), as well as emperors' speeches. In the *Annals* he writes, referring to the Great Fire of Rome, "Nero fastened the guilt and inflicted the most exquisite tortures on a class hated for their abominations, called Christians by the populace. Christus (*sic*), from whom the name had its origin, suffered the extreme penalty during the reign of Tiberius at the hands of one of our procurators, Pontius Pilatus, and a most mischievous superstition, thus checked for the moment, again broke out not only in Judea, the first source of the evil, but even in Rome, where all things hideous and shameful from every part of the world find their centre and become popular."

A painting depicting Christ before Pontius Pilate

When Jesus fatefully entered Jerusalem before the crucifixion, he introduced himself by means of acted parables, announcing judgment for the city and the temple. He entered the city on the back of a donkey, deliberately acting out an old prophecy which said that the new David would appear in that way. Thus he provoked massive political and religious expectation among the people, as both spheres were inseparable at that time. Inevitably, that alerted and alarmed the Roman authorities.

A medieval depiction of Jesus entering Jerusalem

Jesus found Jerusalem seething with revolutionary passion, in direct opposition to his demand to resist evil peacefully. But the city would choose, metaphorically, the revolutionary Barabbas (possibly a character created by Mark) over Jesus the pacifist. He came into conflict with the religious leaders, collaborators of the Roman power, until a critical point when he stormed into the temple of Jerusalem to announce its imminent judgment and future destruction (which actually occurred in the year 70 when some who had heard and seen him were still living).

The demonstration in the temple courtyard caused protests, some in favor, others against, that ended with his arrest and execution on the cross. As if making his presence known, word quickly spread that Jesus had launched an attack in the "Court of the Gentiles" (unlike the "Holy of Holies," the area of the Temple accessible to everyone) on the merchants and bankers serving those seeking to make requisite offerings by overturning tables of the money-changers and the stalls of the pigeon-sellers, crying out, "It is written, My house shall be called a house of prayer; but you are making it a den of robbers" (Matthew 21:13). The following day, the high priests sought to discredit Jesus at the Temple by posing pointed questions concerning the tenets of the Jewish faith, each of which he answered with extraordinary ease and wisdom. When asked by what right he acted as he was doing, he countered by saying that he would answer fully if they would first inform him whether they regarded the baptism of John as divinely inspired or not. Having been eloquently trapped by their own method, if they answered 'Yes,' Jesus would then counter, "Why then did you not believe him?" (Matthew 21:26—27). If they answered 'No,' they risked angering the many followers who venerated John as a prophet. Their answer, "We do not know" elicited the response, "Neither will I tell you by what authority I am doing these things." And when asked "Tell us, then, what you think. Is it lawful to pay taxes to the emperor, or not?" (Matthew 22:17), his answer -- "Give therefore to the emperor the things that are the emperor's, and to God the things that are God's" (Matthew 22:21) -- was taken by many as a subtle condemnation of insincere high-ranking Jews who served the interests of Rome to their own benefit.

According to the Gospels, upon leaving the Temple for the last time, "after two days was the Passover and the Feast of Unleavened Bread." By some accounts, Jesus may have spent the fourth day in Bethany, in the evening in the house of Simon the leper. The fifth day of the "Feast of Unleavened

Bread" commenced with the slaughter of the paschal lamb; that evening Jesus walked to Jerusalem with his twelve disciples for the "Last Supper" Passover meal. That night, he and the twelve gathered in the Garden of Gethsemane, where Jesus was arrested and then taken before the Sanhedrin council for judgment.

While Jesus could have been punished for the disruption caused in the Court of the Gentiles, that would not have resulted in a substantial punishment. The Sanhedrin was more interested in the allegation that Jesus had referred to himself as "the Son of Man sitting at the right hand of the Mighty One and coming on the clouds of Heaven". To the Jewish High Council, that was an extreme blasphemy.

Jesus before the Sanhedrin. Caiaphas is tearing his robe in grief at what he perceived to be Christ's blasphemy.

At about 6:00 a.m. on the sixth day, Jesus was brought before Pilate by the Sanhedrin. The Sanhedrin sought to punish Jesus on account of his blasphemy, but they also knew a Roman prefect would have no interest in punishing a man based on that charge because it would directly involve him in intra-Jewish squabbling. Thus, the Sanhedrin would frame it as Jesus having claimed to be "King of the Jews", a charge that would have been considered treasonous by Roman authorities.

As presented in Biblical accounts, Jesus was brought before Pilate and within three hours' time was at his place of execution. In that space of time, Pilate had heard the charges against him as stated by the high priests of the Sanhedrin ("We have found this man subverting our nation, forbidding the payment of tribute to Caesar, and claiming to be the Messiah, a king"), had personally interrogated him ("Are you king of the Jews?"), ordered him to be flogged, stated that he personally found him guilty of no crime warranting death, but then ultimately gave in to public pressure and condemned Jesus to die by crucifixion.

What can account for Pilate's seemingly contradictory stances? According to Mark, Pilate was initially suspicious of the Sanhedrin for bringing Jesus before him, "for he knew that the chief priests had handed him over because of envy"

(Mark 15:10). In fact, Josephus, who was highly critical of Pilate for the previous incidents with the aqueduct and standards, depicts Pilate as a relatively passive character during the passion story: "At this time there appeared Jesus, a wise man. For he was a doer of startling deeds, a teacher of the people who receive the truth with pleasure. And he gained a following both among many Jews and among many of Greek origin. And when Pilate, because of an accusation made by the leading men among us, condemned him to the cross, those who had loved him previously did not cease to do so. And up until this very day the tribe of Christians, named after him, has not died out."

According to the Gospels of Mark and John, Pilate made clear throughout the process that it was the Sanhedrin who bore responsibility for Christ's fate, repeatedly referring to Jesus as "your king". The most memorable aspect of Pilate's involvement came from the Gospel of Matthew (Matthew 27:24), which states Pilate literally washed his hands to symbolize that he did not consider the blood to be on his hands. While that symbolism was important, it would have meant even more to the crowd because it was a Jewish custom: washing one's hands was a way to wash away perceived impurities, and by doing so Pilate was indicating that he considered Christ's execution an injustice. And had Pilate actually believed Jesus was inciting a revolt, he would have also rounded up the co-conspirators, a step he never took.

In fact, Pilate practiced, observed, and respected several Jewish customs throughout the passion story, as reported by the Gospels. According to John 18:29, Pilate did not force the accusers to come into the Praetorium to lob their charges, because entering a pagan building would have been considered an insult to the Jewish high priests. Just as important, it was Pilate who allowed Jesus to be embalmed and buried before the Sabbath, according to Mark 15:43 and John 19:38.

Pilate took pains not to associate himself with the death of Jesus and demonstrate several ways in which he didn't consider himself accountable, but his decision to not free Jesus when he had the supreme authority to do so made him complicit in what is generally seen as a plot devised by certain members of the Sanhedrin to eliminate Jesus. The tendency of subsequent Christian writers was to increasingly stress the guilt of the Jews and to downplay Pilate's role, as seen in the later Gospels, but the accepted time-table from the trial to the condemnation lasted just three hours. Depictions of Pilate washing his hands and repeatedly passing the blame off on the Sanhedrin distract from the fact that Jesus was almost summarily tried and condemned to be crucified.

Early Christian writers went even further, casting Pilate as an early Christian and/or a figure who should be praised for his role. Early Church fathers like Tertullian asserted Pilate was a Christian, while some of the non-canonical texts in the apocrypha cast Pilate as repudiating the deeds and wishes of the Sanhedrin. St. Augustine of Hippo (354-430) considered Pilate a prophet and said as much in a sermon.

Pilate likely did not believe Jesus deserved to die, and there was clearly political gain to be had by keeping relations with the Sanhedrin smooth, but he was also stuck between a rock and a hard place. By the time the Jewish priests had condemned Jesus, Pilate's position was untenable: if Jesus proved to be guilty of the charges leveled against him and Pilate released him, he would be condoning treason against the Roman Emperor. If Jesus was innocent and Pilate condemned him to death, this would be yet another black mark against him, which would displease his superiors in Rome.

A medieval depiction of Pilate washing his hands

Antonio Ciseris' painting of Pilate displaying Jesus to the crowd

The Gospels also fail to note that Pilate had to deal with other claims about messianic figures in the province, and the brutal manner in which he dispatched one of them. About the same time as Christ's heralded appearance, the Samaritans had also foretold of a messianic figure, the "Taheb," which the Romans feared could incite a revolt. In 36 CE, Pilate sent troops to capture and execute Samaritan leaders who had gathered around a figure claiming to be Moses reincarnate.

Jesus's crucifixion also included a public warning from Pilate, who put the words "The King of the Jews" on the cross. This was another way of saying "this is what happens to your messiahs." (Fredriksen, 1999) Indeed, the fact that Jesus was crucified, not beheaded, burned or other common forms of Roman execution, is proof the Roman authorities wanted to make a public demonstration that not only discouraged people but made clear that Jesus's crime was political. His disciples felt the danger, flew away and abandoned him, leaving their master to die alone, one day before the feast of Passover.

If there's anything that can be said with certainty, it is that Jesus expired in angst and despair. Crucifixion consisted of tying or nailing a man to two wooden beams in the form of a cross, or to a tree. The first reports of crucifixion as a form of punishment came from the historian Herodotus, who wrote that Darius, King of Persia and Pharaoh of Egypt (512-485 BCE), crucified 3,000 people in Babylon. Julius Caesar watched this form of punishment among the Numidians, and several sources report that it was common among the

Carthaginians too. The Romans adopted this form of capital punishment but reserved it for the most serious of criminals—pirates, revolutionaries, rebels (generally of the lower class), and slaves. Cicero called it *summum supplicium*, the ultimate punishment, worse than being burned alive and decapitation. One of the cruelest aspects of the crucifixion, besides the intense and continuous suffering, sometimes for several days, was the public exposure, and the fact that a funeral and proper burial would be denied, an unimaginable dishonor in the ancient world. The bodies of the crucified were usually left hanging to be devoured by animals, with wild dogs waiting for the right moment beneath the cross.

Once Jesus was dead, a Roman soldier pierced his side with a spear, possibly to end his suffering. John remembers: "When they came to Jesus and saw that he was already dead, they did not break his legs. But one of the soldiers pierced his side with a spear, and immediately blood and water came out" (John 19: 33-34).

Jesus's crucifixion was a traumatic event for his

followers, so much so that the early Church spent years in reflection trying to justify and find meaning for it, especially among the Jews. For the Jews, to think of the crucifixion as an act of the Messiah was, according to Paul the Apostle, "a scandal; and for those who are not Jews, it is foolishness."

It is not clear when the cross became a symbol for Christianity. The oldest representations of Jesus show him not crucified but as a good shepherd performing a miracle, or surrounded by beams of light, similar to the god Apollo. "During the years in which crucifixion remained an immediate and hideous threat, Jesus's followers did not paint a cross - much less [a depiction of the crucifixion] - on the walls [in] the catacombs in Rome as a symbol of hope" (Pagels, 2004).

The exception to this rule is the drawing of a crucified donkey, the so-called "Alexamenos graffito," the oldest representation of Jesus's crucifixion ever found. Clearly a mockery of Christianity, the graffiti was found in an ancient building near the Palatine Hill in Rome. On the left side of the crucified donkey is a man worshiping, and in the lower part, a clumsily executed inscription that reads, "Alaxamenos worships his god." For some scholars, it is proof that people made fun of Christians because they had worshipped a man who had died on the cross. The drawing was made in the 2nd or 3rd century CE. Thus the evidence suggests that, at the time, the cross was still a source of confusion and embarrassment among Christians.

A picture of the graffiti

In the year 132 CE, a revolt, led by Simon bar Kokhba, broke out in Palestine, the second and definitive great Jewish rebellion against Rome. It was initially successful to the extent that the Jews regained control of the land for two years, and Bar Kokhba was proclaimed Messiah by Rabbi Akiva, and coins inscribed "Year 1" were minted to mark the beginning of the new era. Nevertheless, Rome returned two years later with six complete legions (about 30,000 men), devastating Jerusalem and the rest of Judea. The population was exiled, the country was annihilated, and the city of Jerusalem was re-founded under the name of Aelia Capitolina by Hadrian.

Even as Bar Kokhba's rebellion marked the definitive end of the ancient nation of Israel and the dispersion of the Jews, Christianity had already taken root throughout the Greco-Roman world. A century had passed since Jesus's death and Christians had also been expelled from Jerusalem, but it is very likely his followers remembered the exact crucifixion site. It is very probable that even before Bar Kokhba's rebellion, the site had been a place of pilgrimage; in fact, when Emperor Hadrian visited the ruins of Jerusalem, he ordered the construction of a temple dedicated to Venus Aphrodite on the Golgotha.[ii]

A bust of Hadrian

The Crown of Thorns

The attitude toward the hideous instruments of torture behind Jesus's death changed in the 3rd century, when the cult of the scenes of the crucifixion became more common. Probably the oldest representation in mainstream Christianity may be found at the doors of the Basilica of St. Sabina in Rome, completed in 432, which shows Jesus being crucified in the midst of the two rebels.

It depicts them being crucified not on three separate crosses but on a single wooden structure that seems to have been assembled for the three men. The attitudes toward the image of a suffering Jesus, formerly exclusive to heretical groups of the Church, and toward the cross were clearly changing.

The depiction of the crucifixion

Possibly the most influential person behind this new attitude was Empress Flavia Iulia Helena, the mother of Emperor Constantine of Rome. Constantine was the emperor from 306-337. According to Eusebius, a historian of the early

Church and author of the well-known *Ecclesiastical History*, Constantine attributed his triumph at the Battle of the Milvian Bridge to a vision of a cruciform over the sun.[iii] Constantine certainly attributed his triumph to divine intervention, but there are no Christian symbols or crosses in the triumphal arch he erected after the fact. The emperor's tolerance toward the Christian church was, in the opinion of many historians, more a cunning political maneuver than a real conversion. Constantine was, in fact, baptized only while on his deathbed. His interest seems to have been more in tolerance of cults, and in the case of Christianity, to bring an end to the theological quarrels dividing his domains. Constantine's mother, Helena, born in present-day Turkey, was a Christian, so it is probable she was an influence behind Constantine's decree allowing religious freedom and the erection of Christian temples in Palestine.

A bust of Constantine

In 313, the Edict of Milan granted legal status to Christianity in the Roman Empire. In her book about ancient Rome, historian Marta Sordi believes this measure had more to do with social stability and the obsession Roman culture had with remaining on good terms with all the deities. Constantine considered the Christian god to be the most powerful of all. One cannot underestimate the influence of his mother, Helena Augusta, in this belief and Constantine's edict on the freedom of cults.

Tolerance for Christianity was reflected in major construction activities in old Jerusalem, which, until then, had spent its existence in semi-anonymity as a Greco-Roman city. The so-called travel diary of the Pilgrim of Bordeaux is an interesting testimony, written by an anonymous pilgrim who visited Palestine in 333. The anonymous adventurer describes his passage through several sites mentioned in the Old Testament. He also affirms having seen two statues of Emperor Hadrian, still standing, as well as the remains of the Temple of Jerusalem. The location of Pilate's house and that of Priest Caiaphas were remembered, particularly the Golgotha, which was easy to find, since it had retained that name for centuries. "There, at present, by the command of the Emperor Constantine," wrote the Pilgrim of Bordeaux, "has been built a basilica, that is to say, a church of wondrous beauty, having at the side reservoirs from which water is raised, and a bath behind in which infants are washed." However, he did not mention any relics.

Already, the Christians, now tolerated, had begun to wonder about the locations of relics associated with the Passion, and the historian Eusebius related that Constantine's mother Helena made a journey to the Holy Land with this purpose in mind. The natural destination to begin the archaeological search was the very site the historic event had taken place: the city of Aelia Capitolina, formerly known as Jerusalem.

A contemporary coin depicting Helena

It is not known to historians when or how Helen converted to Christianity. Once Constantine had ingratiated himself with the Christian god and tolerated the practice of the religion, his mother, Helena—considered a saint in the Catholic, Anglican, and Orthodox Churches—received unlimited resources from her son to make a journey to Palestine, and according to tradition, to conduct an archaeological search to locate what was left of the earthly life of Jesus of Nazareth, even though 300 years had passed since his death.

Helena left for the East in 326. In his *Life of Constantine*, Eusebius—who was Helena's contemporary—wrote that the queen was already "advanced in age," about 75 years old, when she set out to visit "this venerable land [of Palestine]; and at the same time to visit the Eastern provinces, cities, and people, with a truly imperial solicitude. As soon, then, as she had rendered true reverence to the ground which the Saviour's feet had trodden, according to the prophetic word that says `Let us worship at the place whereon His feet have stood,' she immediately bequeathed the fruit of her piety to future generations."

In her passage through the land, the empress set up

shelters for the poor, released prisoners, and distributed money, but she also asked the inhabitants of Jerusalem the whereabouts of Jesus's tomb and the spot upon which he had been crucified. Helena was taken to the place where the Christian messiah had been buried. There, she found a temple dedicated to Venus Aphrodite, which she immediately had demolished. Beneath the building, according to Eusebius's *Ecclesiastical History*, were several layers of ground to erase all traces of the tomb. There was "a quantity of earth [they had brought] from a distance with much labor, and covered the entire spot; then having raised this to a moderate height, they paved it with stone, concealing the holy cave beneath this massive mound."

  After ordering all of the materials and the ground upon which the ancient temple of Venus had been built to be thrown as far away as possible, the construction of a new temple began above the cave, which Eusebius does not hesitate to identify as Jesus's tomb. In this same work, the Church historian includes the letter the emperor sent to the Bishop of Jerusalem to inform him of the discovery and ask for his cooperation in the construction of a new temple. Eusebius never mentioned Helena's discovery of the True Cross.

After her two-year trip to Palestine, Helena made official the custom of pilgrimage to the Holy Land, a common practice in medieval Christianity, especially during the Byzantine era. During her stay in Jerusalem, the queen erected an imposing temple at the site she identified as the Ascension of Jesus. However, this would not be the discovery that would make her famous. Besides identifying the most important sites mentioned in the Gospels, Constantine's mother dedicated herself to recover relics and objects associated with Jesus's life. She is credited with finding the most spectacular relic of Christianity under the temple of Venus: the cross upon which Jesus of Nazareth had died, thenceforth known as the True Cross.

A depiction of Helena with the True Cross

Interestingly, Eusebius did not attribute Helena with the discovery of the Holy Sepulchre or the True Cross, only the identification of two other sites - those of the birth and ascension of Jesus, where she ordered two temples erected. It is likely that

Helena visited Palestine after the Temple of the Holy Sepulchre had already been built. Eusebius wrote about Helena's pilgrimage, "His mother…had hastened with youthful alacrity to survey this venerable land…she dedicated two churches to the God whom she adored, one at the grotto which had been the scene of the Savior's birth; the other on the mount of his Ascension." The writings of the time do not point to Helena having discovered the True Cross, but they testify that 20 years after her visit, there was already a Cross on display in Jerusalem, considered to be the historical stake upon which Jesus had died. Jan Willem Drijvers pointed out in 1992 that "the story of Helena's discovery of the Cross originated only fifty years after her death, and must therefore be regarded as historical fiction."

Of course, the True Cross wasn't the only potential relic to be sought after. One of the most prominent items in the Passion story is the Crown of Thorns, which in ancient times was worn by convicted criminals. The relic of the Crown of Thorns from the Cathedral of Notre-Dame is worshipped as a visible sign of Christ's passion, especially during Lent. It unites the worshippers with the sufferings that Jesus endured on the cross before his resurrection on Easter Sunday. Preserved in a gilded crystal reliquary and displayed to the faithful every year on the Fridays of Lent and at a special service on Good Friday, this delicate relic has a long and complicated history. For the past eight centuries, it has been protected in glittering Gothic spaces and venerated in Paris as a tangible, physical symbol of Christ's reign.

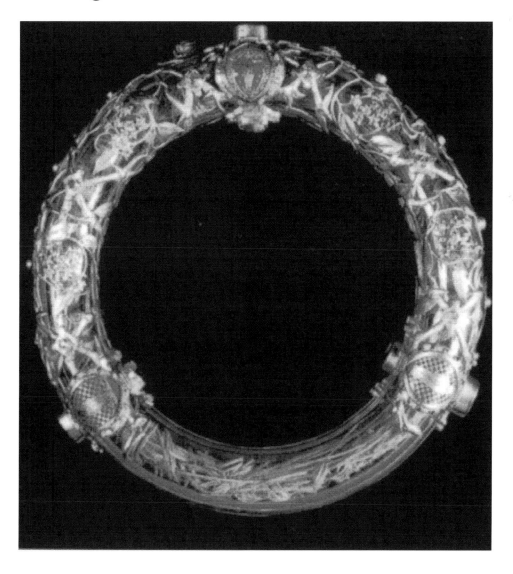

A picture of the relic

El Greco's painting of Christ with the Cross and Crown of Thorns

According to the Biblical accounts, after Jesus was scourged, the Roman soldiers mocked him. They were waiting for the arrival of the administrator, the

Roman governor Pontius Pilate, who alone had the power to condemn Jesus, and until he arrived, they had fun in their own way in his court. They heard that Jesus said that he was a King, and not knowing that his kingdom is not of this world, they mocked him by taking off his upper garment and putting on him a red military raincoat that served as a cloak. Some sat him down on a stone that became a throne, put a reed in his hand instead of a scepter, and on his head a Crown of Thorns.

Apart from the unimaginable torment caused by the thorns pressed into the skull of the already beaten and tortured Christ, the crown that He wore reminds Christians of the humiliation and mockery that the King of Kings had to endure for those whom he came to save, denying his righteous crown of glory and replacing it with a crown of suffering and shame.

The Crown of Thorns in the Gospels is somewhat of a puzzle. Romans, in the time of Jesus, honored the laws, and according to Roman law, they should not mock in the manner of a person sentenced to death on the cross. In fact, the soldiers were to refrain from mocking the convict and his religious beliefs. However, it's hard to interpret the story in the Gospels as an allegory because the Crown of Thorns is mentioned in three of the Gospels as one of the many instruments used while mocking Christ during his trial and punishment (Matthew 27:27-30[3], Mark 15:16-19, and John 19:1-3). In John's account, the Passion narrative is expanded, and Christ is brought before the Roman governor of Judea, Pontius Pilate, to face the multitude while still wearing the Crown of Thorns: "So Pilate then took Jesus and had Him flogged. And the soldiers twisted together a Crown of Thorns and placed it on His head, and put a purple cloak on Him; and they repeatedly came up to Him and said, 'Hail, King of the Jews!' and slapped Him in the face again and again. And then Pilate came out again and said to them, 'See, I am bringing Him out to you so that you will know that I find no grounds at all for charges in His case.' Jesus then came out, wearing

---

[3] Then the soldiers of the governor took Jesus into the common hall, and gathered to him the whole band of soldiers.

And they stripped him, and put on him a scarlet robe.

And when they had platted a Crown of Thorns, they put it upon his head, and a reed in his right hand: and they bowed the knee before him, and mocked him, saying, Hail, King of the Jews?

And they spit upon him, and took the reed, and struck him on the head.

And after that they had mocked him, they took the robe off from him, and put his own raiment on him, and led him away to crucify him.

the Crown of Thorns and the purple robe. And Pilate said to them, 'Behold, the Man!' So, when the chief priests and the officers saw Him, they shouted, saying, 'Crucify, crucify!' Pilate said to them, 'Take Him yourselves and crucify Him; for I find no grounds for charges in His case!' The Jews answered him, 'We have a law, and by that law He ought to die, because He made Himself out to be the Son of God!'"[4]

In the *Golden Legend*, Jacobus de Voragine wrote that the cross on which Jesus Christ died, as well as the Crown of Thorns and other instruments of the Passion, were collected and hidden by some disciples. Around 320, Emperor Constantine's mother, Helena[5], cleared the debris that had accumulated around Golgotha, the hill of crucifixion, in Jerusalem. On that occasion, the

---

[4] "Bible Gateway Passage: John 19, Luke 23, Mark 15, Matthew 27 - New American Standard Bible," Bible Gateway, accessed July 2, 2023, https://www.biblegateway.com/passage/?search=John+19%2CLuke+23%2CMark+15%2CMatthew+27&version=NASB.

[5] Historians believe that Flavia Julia Helena, the full name of the later Holy Empress Helena, was born around 249 in the city of Drepanum, in the Bithynia region of Asia Minor. Her origins remain unknown. It is believed that she belonged to a lower social class, that her father was most likely an innkeeper, and that she met Constantine's father Constantius Chlorus, in the place of today's Izmir in northwestern Turkey.
It is precisely her belonging to a lower class that could explain the assumptions that she was not actually in a worthy marriage with Constantine's father at that time. In the third century, marriage between members of incompatible social classes was not allowed, and Constantius Chlorus was a bodyguard of the emperor and later emperor-overlord. According to historians, Constantine I the Great was Helena's only child.

relics of the Passion would come to light. According to this book, Helena would bring to Rome a part of the cross, a nail, a thorn from the crown, and a fragment of the inscription that Pilate stuck on the cross. Other relics remained in Jerusalem, including the rest of the Crown of Thorns.[6]

When Emperor Constantine fell seriously ill and when, as is believed, he was healed after being baptized, he thought he was not worthy of going on a pilgrimage, so he asked his mother to do it for him. Full of precious life experiences and endlessly grateful to God for her son's healing, Helena did not spare any expenses in trying to locate and exhibit Christian relics in the Holy Land, and thanks in large measure to her pilgrimage, the influence of the Church rapidly grew.

From there, accounts mentioning the Crown of Thorns intermittently pop up. Decades later, in 409, Saint Paulinus of Nola instructed the faithful to venerate the relics of Saint Thorn in the basilica on Mount Zion in Jerusalem, next to the Flagellation Pillar and the Holy Spear. In 591, Gregory of Tours

[6] Richard Stracke, Golden Legend: Invention of the holy cross, accessed June 29, 2023, https://www.christianiconography.info/goldenLegend/inventionHolyCross.htm.

offered the earliest known description of a relic crown: "They say that the Crown of Thorns appears as if it is alive. Every day its leaves seem to wither and every day, they become green again because of divine power."[7]

In 680, the Frankish bishop Arculf allegedly visited it in Jerusalem. If this was the case, it would mean that the relic had not been transferred together with the True Cross and other Passion relics by Emperor Heraclius to Constantinople in 635, as was commonly believed. Moreover, between the 7th and the 11th century, there is no mention of the Crown of Thorns as a venerated relic, although parts of it were purportedly circulating across the Byzantine Empire and Western Europe. Single thorns were embedded in *staurothekes* (reliquaries containing fragments of the cross), found in the collections of relics, or kept as precious gifts. However, no Byzantine source confirmed that the Crown of Thorns was stored in the imperial palace in Constantinople together with the other Passion

---

[7] Dr Emily Guerry, Senior Lecturer in Medieval History, "Notre-Dame: How Christ's Crown of Thorns Has Survived Crusades, Political Upheaval and a Fire (but Only Just)," The Conversation, June 8, 2023, https://theconversation.com/notre-dame-how-christs-crown-of-thorns-has-survived-crusades-political-upheaval-and-a-fire-but-only-just-115731.

relics, and this is especially significant since no mention of the Crown of Thorns is made in *De ceremoniis aulae Byzantinae*, a vital Byzantine work believed to have been written by Emperor Constantine VII Porphyrogennetos in the 10th century. That work, which offers historical information on a range of topics, listed Christ's relics owned by the emperor.[8]

The first reliable trace places it in the Byzantine Empire at the beginning of the 11th century, and it remained there until the 13th century, when Baldwin II, the ruler of the Latin Empire, a short-lived imperial creation founded by the leaders of the Fourth Crusade on the territory conquered from the Byzantine Empire, handed it over to the Venetians as a deposit. According to some sources, he received 13,000 gold coins in exchange for this priceless relic, so he decided to sell it to the French King Louis IX. To prevent it from looking like a worldly purchase, the king arranged to pay off the previous owner's debts, and that's how the relic arrived in France in 1239.[9]

---

[8] Jerzy Pysiak, "The King and the Crown of Thorns: Kingship and the Cult of Relics in Capetian France," OAPEN Home, October 25, 2022, https://library.oapen.org/handle/20.500.12657/59061.

King Louis IX welcomed 29 relics in Villeneuve-l'Archeveque in the Burgundy region of France on August 10, 1239, and then the procession along with the king continued towards Paris. After a few days, the relics arrived in Paris on August 19, 1239, after which the king took off his royal attire and, wearing only a simple tunic with bare feet, continued to the Notre-Dame de Paris Cathedral accompanied by his brother and the rest of the procession, bringing along the Crown of Thorns with them. Louis IX, who would be canonized as a saint himself, had a reliquary, also known as a shrine, constructed for the Crown of Thorns.[10]

[9] "How the Crown of Thorns Ended up at Notre-Dame Cathedral," NCR, accessed June 28, 2023, https://www.ncregister.com/blog/how-the-crown-of-thorns-ended-up-at-notre-dame-cathedral.

[10] EUtouring.com, "Home," The, accessed July 2, 2023, https://www.eutouring.com/crown_of_thorns_notre_dame.html.

A contemporary depiction of Louis IX

During the trip to Paris, numerous thorns were removed to donate to churches and sanctuaries for particularly worthy causes, and other thorns were given by successive French rulers to princes and churches as a sign of friendship. For these reasons, many French and Italian localities boast of having one or more holy thorns.

It is interesting that Croatia, along with France, is

the only country in the world that has an official confirmation of part of the relic from the Holy See, and its holy thorn is in the town of Pag. According to original documents, a holy thorn was brought in 1443 by Brother Ivan Tutnić, to his sister, a nun named Maria, for her solemn monastic vows in the Benedictine monastery in Pag. He also wrote a deed about that gift. The relic itself was kept in the monastery by the Benedictine nuns in a chest with four keys, and the document indicated who was to keep those keys. One key was kept by the Mother Abbess, another was kept by the Municipality of Pag, and a third was by Abbot Tutnić, who later handed it over to a Pag nobleman. The custody of that key became a right of inheritance in that family. The fourth was held by the Pag congregation chapter.

In the spirit and letter of this document from the Holy See, for centuries the people of Pag venerated and observed a festival for what they called "Holy Crowns of the Lord."

The French king was a deeply religious ruler who honored the relics of Christ, and the day the Crown of Thorns was brought to Paris, August 18, was declared a holiday. A stage was built in front of the city walls from which speakers greeted it, and then the Crown of Thorns was placed in the golden reliquary. The crown was not stored in Notre-Dame immediately - at first, it was kept in the also-beautiful Gothic Church of Sainte-Chapelle.[11]

It remained there until the French Revolution at the end of the 18th century, when it became too risky to stay in place. In 1793, an enraged Parisian mob broke into Sainte-Chapelle and destroyed the interior of the chapel. The relics from the shrine were first mocked during a mock procession through the streets of the city and then destroyed. A part of the True Cross from the Byzantine reliquary of Baldwin, which was considered the largest fragment of that relic in the world, was irretrievably lost. So was the handle of Longinus' spear that was allegedly used to pierce Jesus's side during the Passion, along with a piece of linen and a sponge with which Jesus' mouth was moistened while being

---

[11] In 1246, King Louis IX built the Sainte-Chapelle in Paris to house the Crown of Thorns, part of the Holy Cross and other relics such as the Holy Sponge and the Holy Spear. With that alone, it could be said that the Sainte-Chapelle is one big reliquary. The cost of the chapel, which was an unsparing undertaking, was less than a third of the sum given by Louis to Baldwin. In today's terms, the crown was the most expensive collector's item the world had ever seen.

crucified. However, a different part of the True Cross, as well as a holy nail and the Crown of Thorns, were saved from destruction and briefly hidden in the National Library in Paris. In 1804, they finally found their place in the imposing building of Notre-Dame. Emperor Napoleon I visited it, and the Crown of Thorns was put on display every year on Good Friday so that the faithful could see it.

For hundreds of years, the relic remained in Notre-Dame until a fire engulfed the cathedral on April 15, 2017, during which the relic was saved and moved to the Louvre.

The Girdle of the Virgin Mary

The Girdle of the Virgin Mary is the greatest treasure of Mount Athos[12], kept in the Vatopedi monastery.[13] The Girdle of the Virgin is today

---

[12] Athos, a peninsula on the shores of the Aegean Sea, is one of the largest centres of the Orthodox world. On its surface of 335 square kilometers, there are as many as twenty monasteries where about 2,500 monks live. Visitors are also welcome on this holy land, but only those of the male sex because access to women is prohibited by the "Avato" law from the year 442. Only monks have the right to live on the peninsula, which in its entirety is considered one big monastery. Mount Athos in Greece arouses the interest of the public and hides numerous interesting and still undiscovered stories. Mount Athos is a self-governing part of Greece, and it includes monastic forms of life that are divided into six categories, of which isolation in the "winch" is the most difficult form of monastic life. Monasticism is a form of religious life that follows the principles of asceticism, contemplation, self-discipline, spirituality, and detachment from the world.

[13] The Vatopedi Monastery is the second in the hierarchy of monasteries in Mount Athos. It was built in

divided into three parts and is the only precious item preserved from the Virgin's earthly life. According to tradition, the belt was made from camel hair by the mother of Jesus herself.

David Profter's picture of Mount Athos

the second half of the 10th century by three monks: Athanasius, Nicholas, and Anthony, who came from Edirne and were students of St. Athanasius, the founder of monasticism on Athos.

The monastery buildings were built from the 10th to the 19th century. It is a monumental complex of buildings surrounded by high walls, organized in a triangle shape. In the wider courtyard, there is a central temple, a cross-shaped refectory, and many chapels, the most important of which is the Chapel of the Holy Girdle.

In the central temple, the only built-in mosaics on Athos have been preserved, while its frescoes, which were painted in 1312, represent some of the most important monumental collections of the Paleologic revival. It is believed that part of those frescoes was painted by the famous painter from Thessaloniki, Manuel Panselinos. In addition to frescoes and mosaics, the monastery contains several movable icons, manuscripts, and church vessels of unique value. It also has the most holy relics, including the incorruptible ear of St. John Chrysostom, of all other monasteries,.

It is known that at the time of the burial of the Blessed Virgin, the Apostle Thomas[14] was in India, where he was spreading the word of Christ. The Apostle Thomas arrived only on the third day after her repose, and since he was inconsolable and wanted to say goodbye to her, he asked for her grave to be opened. The apostles fulfilled Thomas's request and were amazed: the tomb was empty, but a wonderful fragrance was coming out of it. The apostles began to pray, wanting God to reveal to them where the body of Mary had gone. That day in the evening, the Blessed Virgin appeared before them and greeted them: "Rejoice! I am with you always." According to tradition, on that day, even before appearing before the apostles, the Virgin appeared to the Apostle Thomas while he was praying and grieving. To comfort him, she threw down her belt from heaven, which Thomas then took to the other disciples.[15]

---

[14] Saint Thomas the Apostle baptized the Three Kings. He preached the Gospel, first in Syria and Persia and then in India. At first, Thomas was sad for having to go to such a far country, but the Lord appeared to him and cheered him up. In India, he dedicatedly and with great love preached the Gospel and thus converted many rich and poor to Christianity. Thomas succeeded in founding the church there. He appointed priests and bishops. Saint Thomas died in India. Today, the worshippers at the Christian churches on the Malabar Coast in India are called "Thomas' Christians." In the fourth century, the relics of Saint Thomas were transferred to the city of Edessa and then to Constantinople.

[15] Super User, The dormition of the most holy mother of god, accessed June 29, 2023, https://spclondon.org.uk/en/orthodoxy/332-dormition-virgin-mary.

In the first centuries of Christianity, the Girdle was kept in Jerusalem and during the 4th century in Cappadocia. It was then placed in a golden casket and brought to Constantinople, where it was not taken out until the reign of Leo VI the Wise.[16]

According to tradition, the emperor's wife, Zoe, for inexplicable reasons, suddenly became mentally ill. Due to her severe condition, she experienced a vision in which she believed she would be healed if the Virgin's Girdle was placed on her. It was not possible to reach the Girdle of the Blessed Virgin Mary because it was a shrine that no one was allowed to touch. For that reason, the casket with the Girdle of the Virgin Mary had never been opened during its residence in Constantinople. Nevertheless, the patriarch of Constantinople, at the persistent and humble request of the emperor, opened the coffin and lay the belt on the sick empress. As soon as the Holy Girdle of the Virgin was placed on the body of the sick empress, the

---

[16] During his reign (886-912), the renaissance that started during his father's time continued. Despite this, the Byzantine Empire was facing military defeats by Bulgaria in the Balkans and the Arabs in Sicily - which was completely lost to the empire. Succession problems had already begun during his reign. The Emperor had difficulty in "producing" an heir to the throne. Only one of the first three wives, who all lived a short time, gave birth to a son, and soon he also died. So Leo waited until his new mistress, Zoe, gave birth to a healthy baby boy in 905 before marrying her. This non-canonical fourth marriage divided the church hierarchy.

disease disappeared, to the astonishment of those present. Since that event, the veneration of the Belt of Honor has spread throughout the Christian world.

In the 12th century, during the years of Manuel I Comnenus (1143-1180), the feast celebration of the Holy Girdle on August 31 was officially established. The Holy Girdle was in Constantinople until the 12th century, when it was stolen and transferred to Bulgaria during Isaac's defeat at the hands of the Bulgarian emperor in 1185. Later, it fell into the hands of the Serbs. Prince Lazar of Serbia (1342-1389) presented it to the Vatopedi monastery with a large piece of the Holy Cross. Since then, it has been kept at the altar of the cathedral of this monastery on Mount Athos.

Known to the locals as *Agion Oros*, or the "Holy Mountain," the peninsula today is most famed for its exclusivity, a place that continues to bar all women and their daughters from entry. The fortress-like monasteries scattered amongst the slopes and the clusters of cells clinging to the cliffs are occupied by monks of the Eastern Orthodox Church. Of course, its male-only population is just one aspect of the peninsula's anomalous nature.

Planted on the peninsula's coast is a black Byzantine Cross, a flat, cross-shaped monument with a trinity of flared, wide-armed, Greek crosses in place of its arms and a traditional Christian cross in its center, kissed with rust. It serves as an emblem of the monastic society that resides there, and it delineates the boundary between Mount Athos and the rest of Greece. Entering this hallowed peninsula is like setting foot into a living time capsule, because life here has not changed in well over 1,000 years. Mount Athos is one of only two places on earth (the other being the Mar Saba) that chooses to run on "Byzantine time," meaning Hour 0:00:00 only begins at sundown. Moreover, it is the only territory in the world that flies the Byzantine flag, a regal, sword and cross clutching double-headed eagle set against a rippling canvas of gold.

Of course, to reduce Mount Athos to an antediluvian, single-sex monastic retreat would be an oversimplification of the fascinating history and simple, yet complex culture that has developed on this stunning strip of land. This is a place as mystically mysterious as it is serene, a space abound with treasures, miracles, and spiritual revelations. But for a place where purity and God-fearing devotion apparently reign supreme, it is certainly burdened with its fair share of controversy.

Ironically, the ostensibly anti-woman culture within Athos, as maintained by its present locals, was conceived by a woman. According to the locals, that woman was none other than the mother of Jesus. By their account, in the summer of the year 49, Mary was invited to Cyprus by a post-resurrected Lazarus. To this, she readily agreed and boarded a small boat, but as fate would have it, a dreadful storm struck, steering the helpless vessel to the eastern coast of the Athonite peninsula, close to the present monastery of Iveron. The disoriented, but otherwise unhurt Mary staggered out of the broken boat. As soon as she took in the beauty of her surroundings, the soles of her feet sinking into the toasty sand, all panic and fear melted away. "This mountain is holy ground," she proclaimed to her son, her eyes fixed upon the mist cloaked over the Athonite peak. "Let it now be my portion. Here let me remain for eternity."

What happened next was nothing short of a miracle, one that could only be powered by the heavens. Once Mary started towards the slopes, the splendid temple devoted to Apollo, built on the Athonite summit, crumbled. This triggered a domino effect, and one by one, sculptures of pagan statues and other "false idols" either toppled over or disintegrated. Left standing amidst the rubble was the stone statue of Apollo on the peak of the mountain, which came to life and thundered across the peninsula: "Heed my words – I am a false idol. You must renounce me and come forth to pay tribute to the *Panaghia*, the true mother of God." With that, Apollo self-destructed.

Hermits and villagers alike did as they were ordered and came forth to honor their new matriarch. Each was baptized, cleansed of their pagan sins, and thenceforth tasked with carrying the Christian torch.

Author Gregory Palamas transcribed Mary's promissory speech to her new subjects in the *Life of St. Peter the Athonite*: "In Europe, there is a mountain, very high and very beautiful, which extends towards the south and very deeply into the sea. This is the mountain that I have chosen out of all the earth, and I have decided to make of it the country of the monastic order. I have consecrated it to be henceforth my dwelling: this is why people will call it the 'Holy Mountain.' All who shall come to live there after having decided to fight the battle against the common enemy of the human race will find me at their side throughout their lives…I will be their invincible aid, I will teach them what they must do, and what they must avoid. I myself shall be their tutor, their physician, their nurse. I shall take care to give them both food and the care that their bodies require, and that which is necessary for their souls, to inspire and invigorate them, so they depart not from virtue. And all who finish their lives on this mountain in a spirit of love for God and repentance, I promise to recommend to my Son and God that He accord them complete remission of their sins."

Despite Mary's alleged arrival in the 1st century, Orthodox Christianity did not enter the Athonite mainstream until the advent of the Byzantine Empire. It was only during the Council of Nicaea in

325 that this brand of Christianity was declared the official religion, and governmental headquarters were transferred to Byzantium, which would soon become Constantinople a few years later. The Western Roman Empire collapsed in 476, but its Eastern, predominantly Hellenistic counterpart in the Mediterranean endured for almost another thousand years.

Riveting legends aside, knowledge of Athonite residents between prehistoric times and the 9th century CE is flimsy at best, if only because archaeologists are prohibited from digging or "desecrating" the hallowed land. Some historians believe that the first hermits in Athos were asylum seekers who fled during the Arab incursions into Byzantine territory, while others insist they were Iconodules (those who supported the controversial veneration of religious icons) shunned by Iconoclast emperors. Furthermore, there are the Virgin-deniers who insist that the natives were nonconforming recluses from nearby lands who were simply drawn to the unparalleled, and therefore magnetic solitude that Athos had to offer. Christian monks – some disgruntled by internal ecclesiastical corruptions and others simply looking for deeper spiritual fulfillment – eventually chanced upon the peninsula in the 4th century CE and took to the mountains to erect their new homes. At this stage, the Athonite monks lived hermetically, for the concept of communal monastic societies had only just been inaugurated in the Egyptian desert around this time. The tradition gradually spread across the Middle East before penetrating Europe sometime around the late 7th century or early 8th century.

By the year 843, according to the local 10th century historian Genesios, there was already a primitive, but well-established monastic community on Mount Athos. The community was composed mainly of a sizable group of monks who arrived in the early 700s and were present at the Seventh Ecumenical Council of Nicaea (also referred to as the Second Council of Nicaea) in 787. The conference revolved around the controversial issue of the era: icons and their place in Christian worship. This feud between the Iconodules and the Iconoclasts first arose in 726, when Emperor Leo III demanded the removal of Christ's portrait above Constantinople's Chalke Gate.

By the 950s, the Athonites had already developed a functioning governing system, and even a set of legislation of their own. Seated within the uppermost level of the pyramid was the *Protos* (Premier), the governor of all Athonite monastic communities. The *protos* was charged with the representation of the peninsula in domestic and international affairs, and vested with a slew of managerial powers, such as the appointment and dismissal of abbots. Up until 1312, the *protos* was named by the emperor. All *protos* after the fact were elected by members of the *Iera Epistasia,* or "Holy Administration." This board of monastic executives, in turn, oversaw the *Iera Koinotita,* or "Holy Community," which comprised delegates from each of the peninsula's monasteries.

More titles were added to the *Protaton* in Karyes, the administrative capital of Athos, between the latter half of the 10th and the early 11th centuries. Such posts include the *oikonomos* (household-manager), the *ecclesiarchis* (sacristans), and the *epitiritis* (procurator). The governing body convened in Karyes on three occasions each year – Christmas, Easter, and the Feast of the Koimesis of the Virgin on August 15th) – in conferences called *"synaxes"* to dissect the most pressing and contentious issues.

Although Mount Athos has long been credited as the location where the Girdle is stored, there is also a version of history that claims it remained in the Holy Land until the 12th century, when a merchant from Prato, while visiting the Holy Land, married the daughter of the priest who held it in custody. The merchant and his new wife brought the relic back with them to Italy, and upon the death of the merchant, it was given to the city's cathedral. After a canon from Prato's historical rival, nearby Pistoia, attempted to steal the relic in 1312, a new chapel was built in the Duomo to keep it safe, where it remains to this day. It is exhibited for the veneration of the faithful five times a year: on Easter, on May 1st, on the Assumption and Nativity of the Virgin, and on Christmas Day. A special pulpit was built on the outside of Prato cathedral for these occasions by Donatello in the 1430s since the crowds of pilgrims who came to see it were frequently too large to fit within the cathedral itself.

In the year 1351, the city of Prato became part of the territory of the Republic of Florence. From that point, representations of St. Thomas with the belt became a common feature of Florentine paintings of the Assumption, and on the strength of Florentine influence on the Renaissance generally, the motif passed first to the rest of Italy, and thence to other parts of Europe. Several references to the various traditions described appear in one of the most beautiful examples of this motif: the Oddi Altarpiece by the great Raphael Sanzio. It was painted in 1502 and 1503, when the artist was only 19 years old, and is now kept in the Painting Gallery of the Vatican Museum.[17]

[17] "The Holy Belt of the Virgin, a Relic of the Assumption," New Liturgical Movement, accessed July 2, 2023, https://www.newliturgicalmovement.org/2013/08/the-holy-belt-of-virgin-relic-of.html.

A picture of part of the altarpiece

In the years of Ottoman rule, the monastic brotherhood went on trips to Crete, Macedonia, Thrace, Constantinople, and Asia Minor to consecrate and support the Greek people and save them from the plagues that were raging. Many miracles and healings took place while carrying the Holy Girdle.

The brothers of the Vatopedi monastery were guests in the house of a priest in Aino. The priest's wife took part, secretly wearing the Girdle on that occasion. When the brothers boarded the ship, even though the sea was calm, they could not set sail. Astonished by this, the priest's wife felt that it was because of her sin and returned a part of the Holy Girdle to the brothers. As she did so, the ship was able to set sail. After this event, another box was made in which the part that the priest's wife wanted to take for herself is kept.

During the Greek Revolution in 1821, after the request of the Cretans, the fathers transferred the Girdle to Crete as a form of help to the people. However, when the priests were preparing to return, they were arrested by the Ottomans and executed. The Holy Girdle was then bought by the English Consul Domenico Santoni. From Crete, the sacred Girdle was moved to Santorini in the new consul's house. The news spread around the island, and the bishop informed the Vatopedi Brotherhood. The consul asked for a large sum of money and the people, although suffering, managed to collect the requested money, and thus, the belt was returned to

Vatopedi. However, what happened in Aino with the priest's wife also happened to the consul's wife. She secretly cut off a part of the Holy Girdle from her husband, which caused the consul to die suddenly and her mother and sister to become seriously ill. For this reason, in 1839, she asked the monastery to send a representative and take over the part of the Holy Girdle that remained with her.

In 1864, the Holy Belt was transferred to Constantinople because of cholera, which was killing the population. When the ship approached the port, the cholera stopped, and those who were already sick recovered. This miracle aroused the sultan's curiosity, so he wanted to kiss the Holy Girdle himself.

During the period when the Holy Girdle was in Constantinople, a Greek resident from Galata requested that it be transferred to his house because his son was seriously ill. When the Girdle arrived at his house, the patient had already died. The priests did not give in to despair. They asked to see the dead man, and when they put the holy Girdle on him, he came back to life.

In 1894, the Holy Girdle was brought to Madito in Asia Minor due to an infestation of locusts that had destroyed forests and fields. When the ship with the Holy Belt arrived at the port, the sky was covered by a cloud of locusts that began to fall into the sea, so the ship was barely anchored. Seeing this miracle, the population enthusiastically chanted, "Lord, have mercy."

In 1915, according to the memoirs of Father Kozma Chrysoulas, the relics of the Mother of God helped to stop an invasion of locusts in the Greek settlement of Neochori. The Girdle was brought there by monks from the Vatopedi monastery. According to the priest's testimony, as soon as the shrine was brought to the village, flocks of birds appeared in the sky and quickly destroyed the locusts. This miracle saved many people from starvation.

In 1957, the inhabitants of the island of Thassos arrived at the monks of Vatopedi monastery. For several years there was no rain, the crops stopped growing, and the drought threatened a terrible famine. People asked to bring the Girdle of the

Virgin to them and save them from this disaster. The monks got ready in a few days. When they sailed from the port, the weather was clear, but when the ship with the shrine approached Thassos, the priests saw there was heavy rain. The weather was such that the monks could not leave the ship and sailed back to Vatopedi.[18]

To this day, the Holy Girdle is credited with working miracles, especially for barren women. They are given a part of the consecrated ribbon on the Holy Girdle, and with the help of faith and prayer, they receive grace from the Lord and give birth.

The Girdle is occasionally brought to other countries so that as many believers as possible can pray in front of the shrine. However, in recent years they rarely take the relics out of the monastery, and the holy fathers do not accept all invitations. So, in recent years, several countries have been rejected, including the United States and Romania.

In 2011, an exception was made for Russia, and in

---

[18] "The Great and Holy Monastery of Vatopaidi," Православие.RU, accessed June 30, 2023, https://pravoslavie.ru/89305.html.

the fall of that year, the Holy Girdle, on the initiative of the Foundation of Saint Andrew the First-Called, was brought to Russia for a whole month. During that time, believers could worship the shrine in 12 cities, including Moscow, Saint Petersburg, Saransk, Yekaterinburg, Vladivostok, and others. It is estimated that more than 3 million pilgrims arrived to see the Girdle.

The Hand of John the Baptist

Of all the Christian martyrs, virtually none can compare to John the Baptist, and one of Christianity's most prized relics is purportedly one of his hands. Naturally, his hand is considered to have immeasurable importance for the entire Christian world because he personally baptized Jesus Christ in the River Jordan. The hand's journey from the martyrdom of John the Baptist up to the present time is so incredible that it almost resembles the script of an *Indiana Jones* movie.

Among the people surrounding the Savior, John the Baptist[19] occupies a unique place due to the way he

---

[19] Saint John is named the Baptist because he baptised Jesus Christ in the Jordan River. He baptised many Christians in the Jordan River, which proves that he existed as a historical figure. Tradition says that John baptised those who repented for not immediately believing in Christianity as well. He lived a

came into the world, his way of life, his role in the baptism of Jesus, and his tragic end. According to the Gospel of Luke, John was born in the time of King Herod the Great as the son of a priest named Zechariah and his wife Elizabeth, pious people who were well on in years and had no children. Luke continues the lovely story about the birth of John as follows:

> "And it came to pass that while Zechariah executed the priest's office before God in the order of his course, according to the custom of the priest's office, his lot was to burn incense when he went into the temple of the Lord. And the whole multitude of the people were praying outside at the time of incense. And there appeared unto him an angel of the Lord, standing on the right side of the altar of incense. And when Zechariah saw him, he was troubled, and fear fell upon him. But the angel said unto him, 'Fear not, Zechariah, for thy prayer is heard, and thy wife Elizabeth shall bear thee a son, and thou shalt call his name

completely ascetic life, feeding exclusively on insects and honey, and was always dressed in camel skin.

John. And thou shalt have joy and gladness, and many shall rejoice at his birth. For he shall be great in the sight of the Lord, and shall drink neither wine nor strong drink, and he shall be filled with the Holy Spirit even from his mother's womb. And many of the children of Israel shall he turn to the Lord their God. And he shall go before Him in the spirit and power of Elijah, to turn the hearts of the fathers to the children, and the disobedient to the wisdom of the just, to make ready a people prepared for the Lord.'

"And Zechariah said unto the angel, 'Whereby shall I know this? For I am an old man, and my wife well stricken in years.'

"And the angel answering, said unto him, 'I am Gabriel who stands in the presence of God, and am sent to speak unto thee and to show thee these glad tidings. And behold, thou shalt be dumb and not able to speak until the day that these things shall be performed, because thou believe not my words which shall be fulfilled in their season.'

"And the people waited for Zechariah, and marvelled that he tarried so long in the temple. And when he came out, he could not speak unto them, and they perceived that he had seen a vision in the temple; for he beckoned unto them and remained speechless. And it came to pass that as soon as the days of his ministry were accomplished, he departed to his own house. And after those days his wife Elizabeth conceived, and hid herself five months, saying, 'Thus hath the Lord dealt with me in the days wherein He looked on me, to take away my reproach among men.'"[20] (Luke 1: 5-25)

Saint John differs from all the other prophets in that, according to tradition, he was lucky enough to be able to show the world "the one he prophesied" with his hand. It is said that the hand of St. John was

[20] "John the Baptist," Livius, accessed July 2, 2023, https://www.livius.org/articles/religion/messiah/messianic-claimant-5-john-the-baptist/.

presented to the people every year on the saint's day. Sometimes that hand appeared outstretched and sometimes contracted. In the first case, it meant a fruitful and abundant year, and in the second, a barren and hungry one.

John the Baptist was highly respected in the Christian world from the beginning. In the Middle Ages, his holiday (Midsummer Day) was called "summer Christmas." One of the largest Christian basilicas, found in Damascus, is dedicated to John the Baptist, and in honor of St. John the Baptist, many churches were built, starting with the Lateran Basilica in Rome, the papal cathedral.

Christians celebrate St. John's feast several times a year. In the Roman Catholic Church, his birth is celebrated as a holiday on June 24, and his martyrdom as a memorial on August 29. The Serbian Orthodox Church celebrates it on January 7, according to the Julian calendar and on January 20, according to the Gregorian calendar. The birthday of St. John is celebrated on July 7 (June 24, according to the Julian calendar) and the day of his death is marked with the Feast of the Cutting (August 29 in

Gregorian, September 11 in Julian).

Believers very often give the name of John to their children, both among the Orthodox and Catholics. Orthodox Christians celebrate the baptism of St. John, and Catholics usually celebrate the name day. In Croatia, the towns Ivanic Grad, Ivanec, Kloštar Ivanic, Sveti Ivan Zelina, Sveti Ivan Žabno, Ivanska, and Ivankovo are named after him. In Bosnia and Herzegovina, in Podmilac near Jajce, there is a large shrine of St. John the Baptist. The Veselinje Monastery and Zagrade Monastery are dedicated to him..

In 2010, on the island of Saint John near Sozopol in Bulgaria, formerly Apollonia, Bulgarian archaeologists found part of the relics of Saint John the Baptist. They were thought to have been irretrievably lost after the Ottoman conquest of Constantinople.

Naturally, John the Baptist's martyrdom is one of the most crucial aspects of his legacy. He was executed by order of Emperor Herod Antipas, and at the request of his wife, Herodias. Herod Antipas,[21]

---

[21] He was appointed tetrarch of Galilee and Perea by the Roman emperor Augustus Caesar. Tetrarch was

the son of Herod the Great (who killed the newborns of Bethlehem at the time of the birth of Jesus), ruled Galilee and Perea at the time Jesus preached. Herod Antipas was married to the daughter of the Arab Prince Areta. Herod banished his lawful wife and took as his mistress Herodias, the wife of his brother Philip, who was still alive. John the Baptist stood up against this lawlessness and attacked Herod and Herodias in public. The ruler did not allow anyone to speak against him, and John soon found himself in prison.

During a party in his court in Sebaste of Galilee, Salome, daughter of Herodias and Philip, danced in front of the guests.[22] Drunk Herod, enraptured by the fire dance, promised the dancer that he would give her whatever she asked for, and she, at the persuasion of her mother, asked for the head of John the Baptist on a platter. Thus, Herod ordered that

---

the title of the ruler of a quarter of the kingdom. Herod is sometimes referred to as King Herod in the New Testament.

He rebuilt the city of Sepphoris, only three miles from Nazareth. Some scholars speculate that Joseph, Jesus' foster father, may have worked on the project as a carpenter.

Herod built a new city for Galilee on the western side of the Sea of Galilee and named it Tiberias, in honor of his patron, the Roman emperor Tiberius Caesar. It had a stadium, hot baths, and an ornate palace. But because it was supposedly built on a Jewish cemetery, many devout Jews refused to enter Tiberias. The Roman Empire sources say that Herod was an able administrator of the province of Galilee and Perea.

[22] "Herod Antipas," Encyclopædia Britannica, June 9, 2023, https://www.britannica.com/biography/Herod-Antipas.

John the Baptist be beheaded in the dungeon and that his head be brought on a platter.

Tradition says that after the execution of John the Baptist by Herod, who rewarded Salome's legendary dance with the saint's head, his decapitated body was buried in the Samaritan city of Sebaste. While visiting the Holy Land, Luke, who was the only apostle and evangelist not directly with Christ, wanted to take the body of the Baptist to Antioch. The people of Sebaste did not want to separate it from the great sanctuary, but they allowed the apostle Luke to take the precious right hand of John, who baptized Christ, to Antioch.

Contrary to the Christian account, historians believe that King Herod Antipas liquidated John because he saw a clear political threat in him. John's execution, like that of Jesus later, was also recorded by the Jewish historian from the 1st century, Josephus. When, after John's execution, Herod's army was destroyed in a battle with the enemy's army, the Jews believed that it was God's punishment. In fact, after John's death, the movement of his followers continued to exist alongside Jesus' movement. It is known that in the 1st century, after Christianity had already begun to spread, parallel to the communities of Christ's followers, there were also communities of John's followers, and they knew only "John's baptism," which is also witnessed in the Acts of the Apostles.

The Apostle Mark has a slightly different story about John's execution:

> "Herod heard of Jesus, for his name was spread abroad. And he said, 'John the Baptist has risen from the dead, and therefore these mighty works show forth themselves in him.'

> "Others said, 'It is Elijah,' and others said, 'It is a prophet, or like one of the prophets.'

> "But when Herod heard of it, he said, 'It is John, whom I beheaded; he has risen from the dead.' For Herod himself had sent forth and laid hold upon John, and had bound him in prison for the sake of Herodias, his brother Philip's wife; for he had married her. For John had said unto Herod, 'It is not

lawful for thee to have thy brother's wife.'

"Therefore Herodias had an inward grudge against him and would have killed him, but she could not; for Herod feared John, knowing that he was a just man and holy, and kept him safe. And when he heard him, he did many things, and heard him gladly.

"And when a convenient day had come, when Herod on his birthday gave a supper for his lords, high officers, and chief officials of Galilee, and when the daughter of the said Herodias came in and danced, and pleased Herod and those who sat with him, the king said unto the damsel, 'Ask of me whatsoever thou wilt, and I will give it to thee.'

"And he swore unto her, 'Whatsoever thou shalt ask of me, I will give it to thee, unto the half of my kingdom.'

"And she went forth and said unto her mother, 'What shall I ask?'

"And Herodias said, 'The head of John the Baptist.'

"And she came back straightway with haste unto the king and asked, saying, 'I will that thou give me at once on a charger the head of John the Baptist.'

"And the king was exceedingly sorry, yet for his oath's sake and for their sakes who sat with him, he would not reject her. And immediately the king sent a *speculator* and commanded John's head to be brought. And he went and beheaded him in prison and brought his head on a charger and gave it to the damsel; and the damsel gave it to her mother. And when John's disciples heard of it, they came and took up his corpse and laid it in a tomb."[23] (Mark 6: 14-29)

With the coming to power of the last emperor from the Constantine dynasty, Julian the Apostate,[24]

---

[23] "John the Baptist," Livius, accessed July 2, 2023, https://www.livius.org/articles/religion/messiah/messianic-claimant-5-john-the-baptist/.

[24] Julian Flavius Claudius ascended the throne of the Roman Empire in the middle of the 4th century, intending to turn back the clock. He ruled for only eighteen months (361–363 AD) before losing his life in a military campaign against Persia. Historians and scientists are divided in their views and opinions

terror arose over Christians and their sanctuaries. Julian, a supporter of pagan polytheism, ordered the destruction of churches, the burning of holy relics and the persecution of Christians not seen since the time of the last polytheistic rulers on the Roman throne. The Baptist's body was also burned in Sebaste, together with the church that was built over his remains.

But Blessed Symeon Metaphrastes also writes that it was not the Baptist's body that was burned, but another body placed in its place. Because, says Metaphrastes, the patriarch of Jerusalem, having learned earlier about the order of the persecutor, secretly took the relics of the Baptist from the grave and sent them to Alexandria for safekeeping. Instead of it, he put the bones of another man in the place of the relics of the Baptist.[25]

---

about Julian. And while some view him from a negative historical perspective because his ideological and religious aspirations experienced a collapse, others consider that his influence represents one of the critical points in the history of Christianity.

Julian himself was an almost unique combination of a Roman emperor, a Greek philosopher, a mystic, and a pagan. Therefore, analyzing his appearance on the historical scene from any aspect is not simple at all. Although some sources portray Julian as a capable military leader, a fair and honest ruler, in the church's memory he is known as Apostate due to his ardent paganism and open antagonism that he displayed towards Christianity. On the other hand, Julian was a role model for pagan writers, as were the rhetorician and philosopher Livanius and historian Ammianus Marcellinus in the fourth century, , and the historian Zosimus in the 6th century.

[25] Kostasadmin, "St. John the Baptist," The Orthodox Path, December 12, 2021, https://www.orthodoxpath.org/saints-and-elders-lives/st-john-the-baptist/.

The revenge of the emperor was stopped by Julian's sudden death in battle, and Christianity could breathe a sigh of relief.

When the Ottomans conquered Antioch, a resourceful Christian Job, with the help of cunning and courage, managed to transfer the hand of the Baptist to Constantinople. It was on the eve of the Epiphany in 956, when the Byzantine Empire was ruled by the scholar-emperor Constantine VII Porphyrogenites.

After 1204, the story of the Baptist's right hand became more and more convoluted and less and less reliable. It seems that the relic had undergone minor fragmentation even before the first fall of Constantinople.[26] During that time, two fingers were already separated from the hand, one which was mentioned by Anthony of Novgorod as early as 1200 as being in Stoudios Monastery. Today, that finger is kept in the Ottoman Museum in Istanbul.

The second finger, however, is kept in Siena. The Siena relic of the Baptist's right hand has a short

[26] Danica Popovic, "The Siena Relic of John the Baptist's Right Arm, Zograf 41," Academia.edu, May 11, 2018,
https://www.academia.edu/36611376/The_Siena_relic_of_John_the_Baptists_right_arm_Zograf_41.

and quite meager history of previous research, no doubt disproportionate to its importance. One of the main reasons is the fact that even today, after so many centuries, the relic has not become a museum exhibit but enjoys the status of a cultic object to which the faithful of Siena come to pay reverence.[27]

After the fall of the Byzantine and Serbian empires, the relics were taken by Jelena, the wife of Đurađ, the son of the despot Lazar Branković, to her father, Thomas Palaiologos in Morea. And when the brother of the last Byzantine emperor, Constantine XI Dragaš, was driven from his throne by the Ottomans, he fled to Italy in 1461 under the protection of Pope Pius XI. As a gift to him, he brought this shrine, which Pius XI, being born in Siena, gave to the temple of St. Maria. With the highest honors, the hand was placed in the court imperial church, and from there, it arrived in the possession of the Maltese Order of St. John of Jerusalem[28], whose founders were the crusader

---

[27] Danica Popovic, "The Siena Relic of John the Baptist's Right Arm, Zograf 41," Academia.edu, May 11, 2018, https://www.academia.edu/36611376/The_Siena_relic_of_John_the_Baptists_right_arm_Zograf_41.

[28] The Knights of Malta were founded in 1050 when a hospital for pilgrims was built in Jerusalem, and they were recognized as a religious order in 1113 when their hospital in Jerusalem became an institution of the Holy See with the right to appoint a grand master. The order lost its territory in Jerusalem, from where it moved to Rhodes, and then to Malta in 1530, where they remained a bastion of Christianity that the Turks were unable to conquer. That is why Napoleon expelled them in 1798 by deception and

knights. One version says they received it as a gift from the powerful Ottoman Sultan Bayezid II, who gave it to the island of Rhodes in 1484. Suleiman I conquered the island in 1522, during which the relic was taken to Malta, where it stayed for 250 years until Napoleon conquered the island in 1798.[29]

In 1798, the hand arrived in Russia, and the Russian Emperor Paul Petrovitch Romanov ceded the Vorontsovsky Castle in St. Petersburg to the knights. It was there that they housed their convent and built the Catholic Church of St. John of Jerusalem, where they placed the hand of John the Baptist. As a sign of gratitude, the emperor received from the knights the title of Grandmaster and a unique spiritual-diplomatic gift: the hand of Saint John, a piece of the True Cross, and an icon of the Virgin of Philermos. But the emperor's mercy was short-lived. Paul's successor, Alexander I, who was in power when the Russians beat back Napoleon's invasion, refused the title of Grand Master and abolished the Maltese Order in Russia, in 1817. The

---

without firing a single shot, attacking the island knowing the rule of the Maltese not to fight against Christians.

[29] Another story says it came into possession of the Maltese Order during the great robbery following the first fall of Constantinople in 1204, which was conquered by the Crusaders.

shrines were kept in Gatchina, and the Synod of the Russian Orthodox Church established October 25 as the day when the relics' transfer to Russia is celebrated.

The hand of John the Baptist was kept in Imperial Russia until the October Revolution, when Maria Fyodorovna, the Danish princess and mother of Tsar Nicholas II, took it to Copenhagen. When she was safe, in an agreement with Metropolitan Antoni Hrapavicki, she decided to hand over the relic to the royal house of Karađorđević. Bagration Timuras brought the hand of Saint John to Belgrade at the end of the 1920s. As a sign of gratitude, King Aleksandar Karađorđević offered Timuras a high rank in the Yugoslav army. The Russian did not want that, instead demanding that he start his education from the beginning and finish the Military Academy first. Later he became an officer in the king's guard.

In 1941, when the government and King Petar began to retreat before the arrival of the Wehrmacht, the hand of St. John was taken from Belgrade and hidden, together with other valuables, in the Ostrog monastery. Why the king did not take it farther has never been officially explained.

After the end of World War II, since it was not known where the saint's hand was, various stories began to circulate. One of those started in Spain, and it was believed the Luftwaffe chief, Hermann Göring himself, had the hand. He allegedly gave it to Hitler, and after that, it somehow ended up in Spain.

When Tomislav Karađorđević was in Madrid in 1955, a group of people visited him and offered to buy the hand for a million pounds. However, the relic was in Yugoslavia the whole time.

After the end of World War II, one of the monks from the Ostrog monastery told the new communist authorities what was in their cells. In the strictest secrecy, the hand of John the Baptist and a part of the True Cross were handed over from the vault to the Metropolitan Danilo Dajković to the Cetinje monastery, and the icon of the Blessed Virgin, Our Lady of Philermos[30], was handed over to the State

---

[30] It is considered the oldest preserved image of the Virgin. Legend has it that he painted Luke the Evangelist based on a living model in the middle of the first century.
Its historical path can be traced back to 1395, when the Knights of Malta brought it to the island of

Museum in Cetinje in 1978, where it is located today. The hand and part of the True Cross were initially stored in the treasury of the Cetinje monastery. Since 1993, they have been brought out for public presentation, with the relics of St. Peter of Cetinje. They were presented later in the chapel dedicated to St. John the Baptist, as well as the monastery itself.

In 2006, the hand was displayed in many cities in Russia, Belarus, and Ukraine, where the faithful worshipped it.

Rhodes and placed it in the church on Philermos Hill, after which it was named. In 1470, the island was attacked by the Ottomans, and the first big siege lasted four months in 1480. According to records from that time, the victory over the Ottomans was granted by the Virgin Mary. Their victory resounded strongly throughout the Christian world and certainly helped to strengthen the cult of the Virgin and her miraculous powers.

In 1522, Suleiman the Magnificent besieged Rhodes with a huge armada of over 400 ships. Due to the Turkish occupation of the island, the knights transferred the Icon to Italy, and then to Nice. When the Knights of Malta and the Spanish King Charles V agreed to a new seat, the Icon of Our Lady of Philermos was transferred to Malta, in La Valletta, in 1530. Until 1571, the icon was kept in the church of St. Lorenzo. Today, this church bears the name of St. Mary of Victory and was built on the foundations of the church of St. Lorenzo, which burned in the fire. The cause of the fire was a candle that fell on the organ. The wall where the icon was completely burnt down and miraculously, survived the fiery element, and remained undamaged. The Cathedral of St. John was built in 1578, and the icon was kept there for the next 200 years.

After Napoleon's occupation of the island, in 1799, the Knights of Malta took the Icon to Russia and handed it over to the Russian Emperor Paul I. Its metal frame was then replaced with gold and decorated with precious stones. The border consists of a double row of 270 diamonds, and in the space between are trefoils of diamonds and rubies, while the arms of the Maltese cross are made of enamel. By making a frame, the value of this icon as a sacred object increased enormously. This reliquary was made by the most famous imperial goldsmiths during the time of Paul I. In imperial Russia, special annual holidays were dedicated to it.

During the October Revolution, in 1917, it was transferred to Copenhagen, then to Berlin and Belgrade. It has been in Montenegro since 1941.

Questions of Authenticity

When discussing the fascinating history of important Christian relics, artifacts that have had the power to mobilize armies, change the world's borders, seal alliances, and make kings fight, the aspect of their authenticity seems to become less important. Whether they are authentic or not, their history and influence are relevant, but if they are inauthentic medieval fabrications, more than one reader might have the feeling that time has been wasted rehashing a useless history. At the same time, determining the authenticity of the relics, and whether they were the real items that played a role in the life and death of Jesus, is interesting in its own right.

At the outset, it's important to note that during the Middle Ages, it was believed that the relics – a source of protection and symbol of God's favor for the city and its inhabitants – could be objectively authentic (the actual wood to which Jesus was nailed) or tertiary relics (a piece of wood that had come into contact with the original cross). After all, the relics weren't discovered or secured for centuries. This is understandable since the Christian religion, although it coexisted in general terms with the others, suffered sporadic and cruel persecution. The Gospels admit that when Jesus was sent to Golgotha to die, his disciples scattered, leaving him to die alone. To collect chalices and clothing, or to later return for the True Cross or Crown of Thorns must have been the furthest thing on their minds. The inhabitants of Jerusalem were, of course, aware of the precise place of execution, for the Gospels and secular sources agree that Jesus enjoyed great popularity, both among the Jews and the Greeks.

The Golgotha, the place where Jesus died, means "Place of the Skull," which might indicate it was a site designated precisely for crucifixions and sprinkled with human skulls. Biblical scholar John Dominic Crossan explains that the process of crucifixion left the condemned hung from death to the final consequences, until the remains of the dead person fell to the ground. Burial by relatives was specifically prohibited by the authorities (in all of history, only the bones of one crucified person have been found in a tomb, which is the exception confirming the rule).

Walking through the Golgotha and having to navigate piles of skulls and bones must have been a macabre experience, but just as importantly, Jesus would not have been the only one to die on the same cross or be given a crown of thorns.

About 2,000 years later, there are so many churches that claim to have relics that it is impossible to list them all, and as the history of the relics discussed above makes clear, multiple places often claim to have the same relic. Put simply, there can be no question that some must be fakes, a fact that Calvin acknowledged in questioning their authenticity.

In the end, any serious archeologist would recommend caution when passing judgment on the authenticity of ancient Christian relics.

Online Resources

Other books about Christianity by Charles River Editors

Other books about Christian relics on Amazon

Further Reading

"Bible Gateway Passage: John 19, Luke 23, Mark 15, Matthew 27 - New American Standard Bible." Bible Gateway. Accessed July 2, 2023. https://www.biblegateway.com/passage/?search=John+19%2CLuke+23%2CMark+15%2CMatthew+27&version=NASB.

Butterfield, Andrew. "What Remains." The New Republic, June 28, 2023. https://newrepublic.com/article/92804/medieval-christian-art-relics.

Dr. Emily Guerry, Senior Lecturer in Medieval History. "Notre-Dame: How Christ's Crown of Thorns Has Survived Crusades, Political Upheaval and a Fire (but Only Just)." The Conversation, June 8, 2023. https://theconversation.com/notre-dame-how-christs-crown-of-thorns-has-survived-crusades-political-upheaval-and-a-fire-but-only-just-115731.

"Herod Antipas." Encyclopædia Britannica, June 9, 2023. https://www.britannica.com/biography/Herod-Antipas.

Holy scripture and traditions of the Eastern

Orthodox Church. Accessed June 26, 2023. https://gospelfororthodox.files.wordpress.com/2013/03/holy-scripture-and-traditions-of-the-eastern-orthodox-church.pdf.

"How the Crown of Thorns Ended up at Notre-Dame Cathedral." NCR. Accessed June 28, 2023. https://www.ncregister.com/blog/how-the-crown-of-thorns-ended-up-at-notre-dame-cathedral.

"John the Baptist." Livius. Accessed July 2, 2023. https://www.livius.org/articles/religion/messiah/messianic-claimant-5-john-the-baptist/ .

Kostasadmin. "St. John the Baptist." The Orthodox Path, December 12, 2021. https://www.orthodoxpath.org/saints-and-elders-lives/st-john-the-baptist/.

Popovic Danica. "The Siena Relic of John the Baptist's Right Arm, Zograf 41." Academia.edu, May 11, 2018. https://www.academia.edu/36611376/The_Siena_relic_of_John_the_Baptists_right_arm_Zograf_41.

Pysiak, Jerzy. "The King and the Crown of Thorns : Kingship and the Cult of Relics in Capetian

France." OAPEN Home, October 25, 2022. https://library.oapen.org/handle/20.500.12657/59061.

Stracke, Richard. Golden Legend: Invention of the holy cross. Accessed June 29, 2023. https://www.christianiconography.info/goldenLegend/inventionHolyCross.htm.

"The Great and Holy Monastery of Vatopaidi." Православие.RU. Accessed June 30, 2023. https://pravoslavie.ru/89305.html.

"The Holy Belt of the Virgin, a Relic of the Assumption." New Liturgical Movement. Accessed July 2, 2023. https://www.newliturgicalmovement.org/2013/08/the-holy-belt-of-virgin-relic-of.html.

User, Super. The dormition of the most holy mother of god. Accessed June 29, 2023. https://spclondon.org.uk/en/orthodoxy/332-dormition-virgin-mary.

---

[i] There are still disagreements over the so-called James ossuary, whose existence was announced in 2002. The box was discovered in a first century tomb in Jerusalem, and contains the inscription "James, son of Joseph, brother of Jesus," a clear reference to

the man of Nazareth. According to the Gospels and Paul, Jesus had a brother named James (Matthew 13:55), and his father was named Joseph. The age of the ossuary has been confirmed, but there is controversy regarding the authenticity of the second part of the inscription (the "brother of Jesus" segment). In 2012 Israel´s authorities, after a lengthy trial for forgery which admitted several studies by experts, appointed by the Israeli Antiquities Authority, concluded that "no evidence that the artefact is a forgery was found."

[ii] Hadrian also built a temple dedicated to Jupiter where the great Temple of Jerusalem, now in ruins, once stood.

[iii] Eusebius mentions the incident in a later work, called *Life of Constantine*. He does not make reference to the vision in *Ecclesiastical History*.

Printed in Great Britain
by Amazon

489bc046-c774-496d-b174-5a3602de2711R01